Henry S. Hewit

The Relations and Reciprocal Obligations

between the Medical Profession and the educated and cultivated classes:

an oration, delivered before the Alumni Association of the Medical

Department of the University of the City of New York

Henry S. Hewit

The Relations and Reciprocal Obligations
between the Medical Profession and the educated and cultivated classes: an
oration, delivered before the Alumni Association of the Medical Department of the
University of the City of New York

ISBN/EAN: 9783337878504

Printed in Europe, USA, Canada, Australia, Japan

Cover: Foto ©Andreas Hilbeck / pixelio.de

More available books at **www.hansebooks.com**

THE

Relations and Reciprocal Obligations

BETWEEN

THE MEDICAL PROFESSION

AND

The Educated and Cultivated Classes.

- • -

AN ORATION,

Delivered before the Alumni Association of the Medical Department
of the University of the City of New York,

FEBRUARY 23, 1869.

BY HENRY S. HEWIT, M. D.,

(Of the Class of 1847.)

New York:

PUBLISHED BY ORDER OF THE ALUMNI ASSOCIATION.

1868.

THE

Relations and Reciprocal Obligations

BETWEEN

THE MEDICAL PROFESSION

AND

The Educated and Cultivated Classes.

AN ORATION,

Delivered before the Alumni Association of the Medical Department
of the University of the City of New York,

FEBRUARY 23, 1869.

BY HENRY S. HEWIT, M. D.,

(Of the Class of 1847.)

New York:
PUBLISHED BY ORDER OF THE ALUMNI ASSOCIATION.
1869.

OFFICERS

OF THE

Alumni Association of the Medical Department of the University of the City of New York.

————·•·————

President.

SAMUEL S. PURPLE, M. D., New York.

Vice-Presidents.

JAMES B. McGRAW, M. D., Virginia.
DANIEL AYRES, M. D., New York.
SOLOMON S. SATCHWELL, M. D., North Carolina.
HENRY S. HEWIT, M. D., New York.
FREDERICK D. LENTE, M. D., New York.
JAMES R. LEAMING, M. D., New York.

Secretary.

H. MORTIMER BRUSH, M. D., New York.

Treasurer.

CHAS. J. PARDEE, M. D., New York.

College Historian.

H. M. SPRAGUE, M. D., New York.

Orator for 1868.

HENRY S. HEWIT, M. D., New York.

Committee on Nominations and Arrangements.

D. B. St. JOHN ROOSA, M. D., New York.
J. J. HULL, M. D.,   "
Z. E. LEWIS, M. D.,   "
J. H. ANDERSON, M. D.,   "
WILLIAM B. LEWIS, M. D.,   "

A Catalogue of all the Graduates of the College is in course of preparation. Any information or funds therefor may be sent to Dr. H. M. Brush, No. 7 West Forty Sixth Street, New York.

ORATION.

—•—

. UNITED in the same pursuits, animated by similar sentiments, actuated by a common impulse, surrounded by the same difficulties and perils, and cheered by the same rewards and anticipations, we have called a halt in the march of our lives, and laid down for a moment the burdens we are accustomed to bear, in order to assemble beneath the roof tree of the University, around the council fire of our college, before that altar at whose foot we watched and prayed ere we donned our knightly armor.

The motive power which brings together those of accordant opinions, is not always nor invariably to annunciate truth or combat error, but oftentimes to indulge the communion of affection and the reciprocation of feeling, to obtain by mutual encouragement a more established spirit in doubt, gloom, and despondency; and confidence, fortitude, and hope, in view of inevitable trials, toils, and dangers.

It is in obedience to this imperative instinct which nature has implanted, that we, my brethren of the Medical Department of the University of the City of New York, have associated ourselves in an organization,—that we have met on this auspicious Anniversary, to rehearse the past and consider the future,—that we are impelled to grasp each other's hands, and look into one another's faces, and from our inmost souls diffuse and receive the consolation of generous confidence, fraternal sympathy, and cordial good-will,—while we offer *Alma Mater felix et proles*, venerable but youthful, the tribute, which is so justly her due, of homage, reverence, and love.

It would be supererogation, after the elegant and comprehensive *resumé* of the salient points in the history and *personnel* of this College, given last year by her distinguished alumnus, Prof. Elliot, to attempt a similar sketch in any detail. The events of her earlier years are fresh in the minds of most of us, and she is still too young, and the jarring interests of the present moment too obtrusive, perhaps, to render possible anything like historical impartiality.

We may, however, be permitted to recall for an instant the figures of those eminent men who laid broad and deep the foundation upon which her noble superstructure reposes.

Revene, graceful and classical; Pattison, enthusiastic and eccentric; Swett, cut off in the bloom of an unfulfilled promise; and Mott, whose plastic touch raised horrid surgery to a fine art, and consecrated its terrible but angelic beneficence and beauty a household thought and word.

We may even be pardoned if we pay the honors of a marching salute to some of the more illustrious living representatives of her graduates and professors, who are still faithful to their former allegiance, or illuminating other spheres with the radiance enkindled at her shrine :

Van Buren, who has superadded philosophic breadth and method, and scholar-like research and depth, to the tact and finish of the master's hand.

Draper, whose Homeric pen has emblazoned and made epic the page of our country's history most fraught with wonder and with glory.

Darling, to whose instructed eye the inmost recesses of our vital frame are as the face of a man to his friend.

Elliot, the Mæcenas of this new Augustan age, whose name and fame are dearer and more precious to the New World than are the name and fame of Simpson to the Old.

Clymer, who whilom stood at the portal through which aspirants for professional power and position had to pass, and whose awful front, like the frown of Jove, drove back affrighted the ignorant and unworthy, and whose learning, labor, and taste enrich and adorn contemporary medical literature.

Dickson, whose correctness of observation is associated with such remarkable beauty of expression.

Hammond, who gave so powerful an impetus to original investigation, and who successfully marshaled the forces of the profession to encounter the tremendous catastrophies of the recent political convulsion. We might speak of the military and medical worth, virtue, and courage of John Moore, of Gouley, whose cutting is like the painting of a painter or the chiseling of a sculptor ; of Post,* who has carried the skill and learning of the West to the cradle of science and revelation in the East; but as we go on, the associations of the present gather about us thick and fast, and recollections of the past come thronging and crowding upon the memory, like the pale shades which struggled for room on board the bark of the grim ferryman of Acheron.

We will, then, with your permission, detach ourselves from these fascinating and seductive reflections and reminiscences, and hasten to discuss during the period of our brief reunion, some of the relations and reciprocal obligations between the profession of medicine and the intellectual and cultivated classes of an age or country, more especially with reference to the present age, our own country, and republican form of government.

That medicine occupies in all respects its proper place, exerts its legitimate influence, and fulfills its destiny, will hardly be affirmed. That the relations between the profession of medicine and the intellectual and cultivated classes, and between the schools of medicine and the colleges devoted to preliminary education, are not correct, reciprocal, and satisfactory, will still less admit of denial. We are painfully conscious that due weight and authority are not accorded to medical wisdom and experience, on the part of society at large, and as represented in its aspects of legislation, government, current literature, and

---

* Prof. Geo. E. Post, son of the distinguished Professor of Surgery in the University. Dr. Post, Jr., is Professor of Surgery in Beyrout, Syria.

domestic and social discipline. Legitimate medicine does not receive that cordial recognition either in manners, letters, conversation, and the press, which her manifold services to science, religion, the arts, learning, humanity, and true civilization entitle her to expect, and which she must receive as a voluntary tribute of justice to substantiated claims, before she can accomplish her work and do all that pertains to her sphere of duty and range of ability and obligation.

The narrow view which ascribes to the profession as its only business, lopping offending limbs, counting accelerated pulses, and prescribing physic, has no place in our present consideration, although we are far from undervaluing the humblest duties of the physician, and consider nothing that is human foreign to our thoughts or beneath our notice.

Our immediate concern is now, however, with medicine in its broad and comprehensive character, as one of the forms in which universal truth is expressed, as a channel of personal cultivation, elevation, and perfection, an absolutely essential element of civilization, an expression of philosophy, and ally and co-ordinate force and authority with religion.

As the soul and body are eternal in both form and substance, and inseparable in respect to their final destiny, in like manner philosophy and medicine in the comprehensive meaning of those terms are absolutely indissoluble in their relations. Philosophy, as the intellectual instrument by which the soul apprehends phenomena, estimates their value, and judges of truth and what purports to be true, is necessarily indispensable to medical wisdom as to every other form of wisdom or knowledge. It is necessary to assume this principle to sustain the position we have taken, and design as far as possible to verify, and also to justify the remedy we intend to propose for the evils glanced at, and others, their legitimate fruit and consequence, to which we shall advert. Indeed, it would scarcely seem necessary to enter into an elaborate argument to establish what is apparently obvious and self-evident. We desire, also, in affirming the absolute inter-dependence between philosophy and medicine, to explain certain apparent discrepancies, and assign to their proper origin the errors on both sides which have crept between what appeared to be contradictions in their respective practical developments and affirmations. These errors have prevented the philosophic mind—which is in a greater or less degree the educated mind—from apprehending the rational basis on which medicine rests as a science, and in virtue of which it claims authority; and to divert the medical mind from due consideration of the essential supremacy of philosophy.

While pointing out the errors into which philosophers have been betrayed by ignorance of facts and details, and narrow views, we wish to demonstrate to the medical mind its absolute dependence on philosophy, and the necessity for that species of culture which shall enable it to interpret facts, correctly, gather the fruits of experience, and combine, compare, and generalize the results of diverse forms and methods of observation and experimentation, in order to arrive at the unity and simplicity of absolute truth.

In asserting the necessary and supreme authority of philosophy, we do not intend to condemn or disparage empiricism, but to recognize it as the servant, not the master, and assign it its proper place among the mechanical forces of development. We desire to reunite experiment to reason, and subordinate them to the judgment of the intellect, precisely as, consciously or unconsciously, we sit in judgment upon every item of intelligence conveyed to the mind by the exterior senses. It is unquestionably true that the most exclusive empiric and materialist becomes, if he be a correct observer of phenomena, an exact metaphysician, and practically affirms what he theoretically denies, the subordination of the material to the intellectual, the tangible and perishable to the intangible and permanent; nevertheless, we consider it important, in view of the estrangement between medicine and the intellectual methods as generally understood, to indicate their unity as the ground of a better understanding between the two classes, not only as a great and positive truth, but also with reference to certain results of practical beneficence which will necessarily flow from their recognized and co-operative union.

The tendency of metaphysical science is to exalt the spiritual at the expense of the material, that of the physical sciences, more particularly those especially appertaining to medicine, to degrade the spiritual to the level of the material; in other words, to materialism and rationalism. This divergence, always more or less active, became apparent and influential with the era of experimentation and discovery, and those very agencies which have furnished the basis for the union of science and philosophy, which have demonstrated to science its dependence on philosophy, and given philosophy, so to speak, a foothold upon matter, which have in fact constructed the place to stand on, which Archimides desired in vain, threatened at one time to be the destruction of both mind and matter. It appeared that philosophy was about to resolve matter into nothing, and natural science to exclude the spirit, and that in this dissolution the end of both soul and body would come, and the world expire in the barbarism of heathenism, ignorance and sensuality, and ultimate and consequent stupidity.

The rise and development of histological physiology in medicine, almost simultaneously with the annunciation of the *Giobertian* formula in philosophy, are the elements of the fundamental principle, upon which the mind can rest while making these interesting inquiries. *They subserve the purpose, to say the least, of giving an idea of the method by which the materialism of empiricism and experimentation can be harmonized with the spirituality of the higher philosophy and the truths of revelation, and are a harbinger of the scientific and satisfactory solution of multitudes of difficult problems, vexed questions, and apparently endless disputes.

The formula "*Ens creat existencias,*" as the essential formative element of the human soul; that is, from the first moment of its creation, by its union with a vivified primordial cell, it has the real, active but inchoate knowledge of its own identity and of its Creator, or, in other words, knows itself to exist and God to be, and the cell, by its union with the soul, capable, by spontaneous evolution, of development, not only into the perfect man, but into an eternal entity, afford an illustration of this union, no less mysterious and sublime than lucid, simple, and complete. It enables the mind to grasp the tremendous thought contained in the Incarnation. It demonstrates the essential unity between the experimental and the intellectual methods, the abstract and the concrete, the real and the ideal; between science and philosophy, and, with the element of faith suspended, affords a glimpse of the realization of our immortal destiny.

It is in view of these principles that we affirm that medicine should be interpreted by philosophy, and that philosophy, so long as the intelligence is trammeled by the accidents of matter, must depend for the accuracy of her information upon experiment and induction.

It is in this view also that we animadvert upon the neglect of purely intellectual culture on the part of the profession, and insist upon a higher order of education than has of later years been considered important.

We do not hesitate to say that unless our culture is improved, our relations with the intellectual and cultivated classes reestablished, unless medicine proclaims herself the ally and champion of learning and intellectual authority, we shall not only cease to advance in the direction of pure induction, but shall lose even the splendid results of a sound empiricism, which exalts to-day so many names in our own and other countries, and sheds such lustre upon the medical epoch in which we have the happiness to live.

The relations of medicine to heathen civilization, philosophy, and superstition, its irresistible tendency to false mysticism, and still falser materialism, and its painful and imperfect elaboration of the practical truths it discovered are most interesting subjects of inquiry, both in their essential relations, and their bearing upon the investigations, deductions, and conclusions of modern times.

The ancient mind had the germs of every modern demonstration, and held as primitive truths derived from the tradition of original revelation, much that modern science has simply explained and made practically intelligible.

But it was the light which came incarnate into the world, which vivified these germs of original truth, and enabled philosophy, science, and virtue to assume their places as the controlling agencies of all legitimate and permanent development.

Medicine felt at once the stimulus of a new motive, that of supernatural charity, and began the career which has reached the glorious results of the present day.

The relations between medicine and monasticism and Christian mysticism are equally interesting, and more important, inasmuch as the truths they embraced were always harmonious and tending toward unity and mutual illustration and solution. Their apparent contradictions and animosities were between individuals and imperfect methods, and arose from the want of a correct system of practical experiment, and observation the inevitable concomitant of the age, and circumstances of the period. Their struggles and combats were with windmills, or between champions, who saw each only his own side of the shield.

In the earlier period of the modern development of the sciences, all that was known of medicine was part of the education of every man aspiring to the title of learned. As the monasteries were the centres for the preservation and diffusion of knowledge, and as one of their prime functions was to mitigate the asperities of the age of the ' iron-clad man,' it naturally fell out that the clergy became the repositories of medical knowledge and the principal physicians. The tendency of their studies and sacerdotal character and habits was to elevate medicine in its philosophic aspect, but to depreciate it as an art. The importance which in those days was attached to the soul of man asserted its influence, and prayer and the sacraments held a more important place in the treatment of disease than human skill or material remedies. The eternal life of the patient was considered at least as important as the preservation of his temporal life. It is, or rather was, the fashion to scoff at those holy men, and impugn an age for darkness, which manifested such ardent attachment for the light eternal.

While we studiously avoid anything in the least degree trenching upon the domain of theological polemics, we may venture to say, that the medico-religious practices of the Middle Ages were at least as respectable as modern spiritism, clairvoyance, phrenology, and the doctrine of the infinitesimal.

We may also, with much diffidence, presume to affirm that if the monks had known a little more about practical medicine, they would have been no less holy men, and at the same time far better physicians.

The tendency of the manners of feudal and ante-feudal times, to consider all personal acts or services as menial and associated with slavery degraded the mechanical departments of medicine, and by the interposition of this obstacle between philosophy and practical experiment retarded the progress they invariably make when associated.

This cause kept surgery for so long a period in a low and ignoble position. It obstinately opposed every step of its progress, and still exerts its malign influence, even in this most innovating and expanding era.

The sigh of old Ambrose Paré comes trembling down the centuries to touch a responsive chord in the breast of every military surgeon : sleepless, because he had no boiling oil. How near to and yet how distant was his correct mind from the truth of one of the essential dangers of gun-shot wounds, and how correct was his deduction, accidentally enforced, of the superiority of reparative over perturbative treatment.

The progress of surgery was either the result of accident and lucky adventure, or accompanied and retarded by violent and irrational struggles, arising from the dread which unpractical philosophy always has of change and innovation. *Quieta non movere* has damaged other causes than ours. But genius, discovery, accident, and more than all, necessity, combined to raise surgery above its degraded position, and ere long its professors began to dispute pre-eminence with the elegant, and accomplished, and exclusive physician. Anatomy contributed certainty of method, with skill and precision in execution, chemistry taking its rise in the hermetic philosophy and the black art, assumed the state and character of a science.

Anatomy having furnished surgery with the knowledge necessary for its mechanical procedures, extended its researches, and aided by chemistry, experiment, and new and improved instruments, began to develop physiology, and give it also the character of a science. Pathology and histology followed in due sequence.

The new geographical discoveries furnished multitudes of remedies for the cure of disease. Discovery, experiment, activity, reacted upon practice ; and the profession of medicine emerged from darkness, doubt, obscurity, and much absurdity—intelligent, rational, accomplished, candid, and capable of infinite expansion and development. Diagnosis became precise, and treatment effective.

The cause and prevention of diseases have risen into scientific accuracy and national importance, and hygiene is a recognized function of government.

It was not possible that the class which had possessed the power could behold the rise and progress of an apparently independent and in some respects superior authority without jealousy and opposition.

The quarrel has never been between philosophy and experiment, between religion and medicine, between the authority of the church and the authority of the profession, but between individuals and partisans. It has always been the windmill and shield controversy. It is not surprising that the clergy and the schoolmen looked with distrust and alarm at some of the new methods. Alchemy and avarice gave a devilish character to chemistry. Dissection was associated with the heretical notion of the impurity of matter, and monstrous fables of ghouls, gins, vampires, man-eaters, and demons ; and physiology with impiety, rationalism, and the baldest materialism.

The confidence of the physician was construed as in some sort impugning the divine power and opposing the immutable decrees of Providence. Physicians seldom or never impious, but often skeptical and infidel, inflated with the pride of discovery and intoxicated by the applause of success, retaliated with sarcasm and insult the cautious and sometimes spiteful and meddlesome interference of their former allies, associates, and masters.

Pride of experiment, and imperfect scholastic discipline and training rejected the *a priori* dicta of philosophy. Empiricism, conducted without the co-ordinating direction and harmonizing influence of philosophy, betrayed its disciples into real and apparent contradictions and immature generalizations with the result of violent and persistent quarrels between individuals and sects, thereby exposing medicine to the shafts of wit and ridicule of those scoffers of every age, who, if they serve no other purpose, point out and correct the faults and follies of the wise and virtuous.

Ridicule is to assumption and crude pretension what fire is to gold. That which can not survive ridicule is not fit to live.

But medicine has survived opposition, opprobrium, and ridicule. The surgeon has risen to the same level as that attained by the philosophic physician; the bleeder and barber of the Middle Ages is the gentleman, the knight, and the chevalier of the present; and the humble leech of Pepin or Charlemange, of Charles the Bald and Philip the Fair, is the baron of the first empire and the senator of Napoleon III. The basin has been exchanged for the cross and medal, and the painted stick for the surgeon's sword.

Medicine has in a great degree reconciled its apparent discrepancies. On almost every important principle the medical mind is a unit. There is no conflict between theology and medical science. The authoritative expressions of religion recognize and encourage every species and form of investigation in the interest of scientific discovery. The Author of revelation and the Creator of all things has nothing to fear from the intelligent and critical examination of his works. Advance, discovery, and correct generalization are going at a rate so rapid as to tax the ability of the swiftest and most acute intelligence to keep pace with them. The profession is certain on many points, and on all is prepared to speak with a degree of authority, and to submit the evidences upon which its apodictic declarations are based.

It is not our purpose to produce and marshal the facts to sustain this assertion, but to notify the intellectual and cultivated classes, the heads of colleges, the leaders of public opinion, *literati* authors, professors, and able editors, that we are prepared to vindicate this standard and to assume all the obligations and responsibilities which it implies, and to require from them a corresponding fidelity to social and medical justice and co-operation for the common welfare.

It would seem proper, however, that we illustrate the divergence between medicine and society by a few obvious and striking examples.

The newspaper press, which is rather the reflection of public opinion than its leader or guide, is, to a great extent, conducted by able and clever men, many of whom are graduates of colleges, and not a few possessing a very high degree of mental ability and cultivation. As the power is in the people, and the press is the expression of that power, the press becomes, in our order, the First Estate.

If the relations between the profession of medicine and the

press were cordial; if there were a correct understanding between the learned doctors and the able editors, and if they both had passed together through the same system of preliminary education; if the ethics of medicine were understood and their personal relations those of a good and established society, would it be possible for the press, with a few honorable exceptions, to seize every occasion to disparage the legitimate profession? Would it be so reserved in its award of praise, so liberal in its application of censure? But, still worse, would these able, accomplished, refined, elegant, and witty gentlemen sell their space for public announcements, in unmistakable terms, of offers to perpetrate crimes which strike at the root of society, which undermine public health, which corrupt social morals, which relegate our era to the foulest periods of Assyrian, Babylonian, and Græco-Roman decomposition; which degrade our manners and civilization below Herculaneum and Pompeii, and sink them to a level with Sodom? Would the religious press (save the mark!) sell column after column to the manufacturers and venders of patent and secret combinations of drugs and poisons, which are either frauds in their nature and intent, or the vehicles of concealed but powerful elements, whose applicability can only occur in fortuitous and occasional coincidences between remedy and disease, while too frequently they subserve the purpose of vicious indulgences, in comparison with which ordinary spirit drinking is a prudent, praiseworthy, wholesome, and highly moral practice.

If these powerful and influential agencies recognized in medicine an authoritative organization, understood the ethics of the profession as based on natural justice and vindicated by common law and religion, would it be possible for them to sanction, aid, abet, and perpetrate these outrages upon an equally learned and respectable co-ordinate body? Would they pander to vices in one column which they denounce in another, and both alike for money? It is as difficult for us to understand it as it was for the good but simple-minded Genii to comprehend how the traveler could blow hot and cold out of the same mouth, and with the same breath.

How is it possible for them to offer such an illustration of the power of avarice and the stupidity and short-sightedness of temporary self-interest, and such brazen contempt for justice, principle, public decency, and personal honor?

It is not our purpose to discuss at present the more subtle and elegant forms in which the divergence between the profession and the cultivated classes is expressed, or the kind of practitioners who thrive upon the fruits of the discrepancy. There is one mild species of medical immorality and moral insanity which flourishes in an æsthetic, luxurious, and imperfectly educated class, which has been brought into existence as a result of the sudden wealth produced by the application of steam to machinery. This large class, which prefers the excitements of imaginary diseases to other less elegant but scarcely less reprehensible forms of vice; which is flattered by the idea that it is in some sort emancipated from physical laws, and is capable of understanding and directing the occult agencies and powers of incomprehensible dynamics and imponderable dilutions, is so influential and wealthy that it is not surprising that an order of physicians was found to supply its requirements. Both patients and physicians of this numerous and socially respectable community are such excellent witnesses of the authority and pre-eminent value of scientific medicine, that while they serve our purpose of illustration, they merit at our hands, perhaps, compassion rather than contempt.

But the most remarkable example of the depraving influence which the divorce between medicine and philosophy has exerted in undermining the foundations upon which religion, natural justice, respect for human life, the sanctity of the body, social and legal accountability, civilization, and the perpetuation of Christian society must repose, is in the rise and progress, almost unrebuked, of an uncontrollable domestic crime which has for its elements, impurity, suicide, murder, treason, perjury, blasphemy, and sacrilege,—all the attributes of mortal sins against one's self, the State, and God.

Without carrying our illustrations further, which we might easily do, into the domain of periodical literature, the world of fiction, and the flowery region of elegant private society and conversation, we think we have said enough on this point to justify the assumption that a radical divergence does exist, and to vindicate the somewhat trenchant remedy we intend to propose, albeit, with no expectation that it will be a royal road, but simply a means to an end, and, as we believe, the only means.

We have accused the press and society; we are compelled to come before the same bar, that of medical justice, and accuse ourselves.

The splendid discoveries in medicine, its attitude in presence of the other sciences, the magnificent record of the medical departments, both military and civil, both North and South, during the late war, the aspect of the profession as an advocate for humanity and active agent in mitigating the asperities of the conflict, and restoring a good and friendly understanding; the unlimited and incalculable charities of its members, and the eminent social position which so many physicians have attained as the result of skill in practice and personal worth, encourage us to make the plea of guilty in many important particulars without fear of damaging our cause or receiving a severe condemnation.

But it is nevertheless true that the elevation of the profession is exceptional and personal, not general, homogeneous, and characteristic. Under the prevailing system, the results of the present age are liable to be lost in another. The preservation of the fruits of genius, and of learning, culture, and progress, depend upon organizations, not individuals.

The answer to the question. What, then, is the remedy? is so simple that it seems almost like an insult to the understanding to name it.

It is that every man who is pronounced a Doctor in Medicine shall actually be what he purports to be. It is to affirm the necessity of preliminary classical education, or what shall be deemed an equivalent for classical training in preparing the mental soil, and a subsequent exact certification and verification of the amount of knowledge acquired and the degree of perfection attained by the apprehension and assimilation of the sciences taught. We have no right to graduate any man as Doctor in Medicine unless he be capable of *teaching medicine* up to the standard of the highest average intelligence. That the colleges have failed to exact this standard, or even one approaching to it, and our own among the number, is too notoriously true to need assertion.

It is to this source we trace most of the evils of which we complain. The remedy, so far as our profession is concerned, is in our own hands. Let us insist that every candidate for admission to a medical school shall present his diploma from an incorporated college of rank equal to that of Harvard, Yale, Columbia College, or the University, or submit to an examination, and be rated accordingly with reference to subsequent medical degrees. Let medical students be divided into classes with an appropriate curriculum for each class, and let promotion from class to class be made only on examination and certificate. Let the final examination be conducted by paid examiners recommended by the State societies, and appointed by the Governor with the consent of State Senate. Let us establish three degrees, the Licentiate, the Practitioner, and the Doctor in Medicine. The first degree might be given, after three years, as is supposed to be at present the rule, and should correspond to the best members of our graduating classes, such for instance as are found worthy of appointment on the staffs of the metropolitan hospitals. The second degree could be given after two years more, and should require a standard equal to that which the common sense of the profession ascribes to a first-class physician in private life, and should require, as an absolute prerequisite, a graduation at an institution of learning, or an examination equivalent to that required for a degree. The degree of Doctor could be conferred in two years or more thereafter, and should imply the grade of accomplishment which we expect in the professors of our schools and the chief medical officers of our hospitals, leaving out, of course, the exceptional excellencies which are peculiar to individuals, a wide range of experience or extraordinary culture.

Are we asking too much? Has not the public a right to require this at our hands, and to hold us responsible if we come short of it? And is it not the plan substantially which is demanded and advised by the profession, through its most authoritative and dignified representative the "American Medical Association."

A beginning must be made. Why shall not our own College set the example? An *amende* is due the institutions of learning. Why shall not she, the guardian of so much fame and honor, so pre-eminent in her literary and scientific associations, make that *amende*, and take away from her name at least the sarcasm that the degree of M. D. is but a doubtful title of admission to an uncertain and but half-acknowledged position among the liberal and the learned. At least, let us, her alumni and devoted children, pledge ourselves to sustain her by every honorable means in our power, if she will cease to engage in the vulgar and ignoble struggle for large classes and long lists of graduates, and begin to consider the quality rather than the quantity of her vintage.

This view of medical education opens up several avenues, of thought with reference to its effect upon the colleges and the better class of the educated youth of the country ; of the relations of Government with the function of examination and indorsement, and their immediate reflex action upon manners, conversation, social relations, literature, legislation, and legitimate power and influence.

The colleges love learning as the paladin loved his mistress, as *that immortal man* who is the ideal type of the American soldier, patriot, and citizen loves his veracity, as the soul loves her intelligence.

This love of learning is no transient or sordid passion, but the deliberate act of the rational soul ; in fact, the soul's sensible expression of herself in the natural order, as her love of virtue is her highest expression in the supernatural order. The act of fealty, homage, and devotion toward learning which has been proposed, and of which the recognition of the preliminary rights of the colleges is the first and necessary step, will call forth on their part an immediate response of respect, good-will, and encouragement. The ultimate effects of such a recognition of the rights of learning and the obligation of culture are incalculable, and far reaching to the degree of penetrating to the utmost ramifications of thought and the springs of motive, conduct, and action.

If the Doctors of Medicine and the able editors were fellow graduates, if they had participated in youthful friendships, belonged to the same societies, and grasped the hand of faithful and affectionate remembrance at the breaking up of the class, could the latter violate all these implied and express pledges by deliberate, corrupt, and shameful acts, damaging to the honor of medicine, injurious to morality, and fatal to life ? Would the men of letters, the clergy, the poets, the orators, and the *dilettanti* be as likely, to say the least, to espouse the false in medicine ? Would not the improved sentiment, status, and tone of the profession, itself react upon all classes in a manner so pronounced as to produce an immediately recognizable effect upon virtue, morality, health, happiness, longevity, civilization, and general well-being?

The increased power of expression which a higher education affords, the superior class which it fosters, and the ideas thus diffused, would impress themselves upon national character and literature, with the effect of increasing our intellectual importance in the eyes of foreign nations, assisting in the development

of our resources, and become a bond of union between widely
separated divisions, and an element of greatness in the future
position our country is destined to occupy in the new distribu-
tion of power, wealth, and dominion. The relations of the profession to the Government under our system become in this con-
nection both interesting and important. We have suffered and
are suffering the evils of too much individualism ; we are in
danger of falling into the opposite extreme of a too absorbing
centralization. We desire to preserve for ourselves the liberty
of the republic of science, and at the same time enjoy the advant-
ages and protection of wise legislation.

We think it competent for the State societies and the Medical Association to recommend such laws as shall be in harmony
with the spirit of our institutions, and shall have the rational
consent of those they are intended to bind. We would have the
reforms we have indicated, when made, rendered permanent
and effective by legislation. We would infuse such a spirit into
our Government, that it would never again make articles of
prime necessity to suffering humanity contraband of war; we
would inaugurate and perfect the principle of reciprocity between the medical departments of belligerents, and we would
furnish to the State a body of professional men in civil life
capable of being called into active service by the Executive in
any crisis of public calamity, as war or pestilence.

We would separate all questions of quarantine and public
hygiene from the influence of party politics, and place them
under the control of the profession and of legislation, informed
and directed by medical intelligence.

If illustration were wanting of the influence of classical education in forming the medical mind, without mentioning the
scholars and men of letters of our own country, we can point to
the direct influence which University education exercises upon the
thought and style of the higher class of our English cotempora-
ries, and in the wonderful capacity for labor, intelligent thought,
and mental acquisition characteristic of the German mind, and
of which we have so many brilliant examples amongst us.

American acuteness of observation, quickness of apprehension,
and capacity for rapid generalization have given us a development and brilliancy, which, unless fed by labor, study, and
original investigation, must soon expire.

The American mind has for its basis the intense thought, the
logical character, the stern, resolved, though often misguided
and misdirected principles of the Puritan epoch. The quartz
of that rigid, religious, and metaphysical period has been
crushed, its gold extracted, and too often foolishly and lavishly
squandered. The intellectual life of the future must be sus-
tained by crops raised by careful cultivation, subsoil plowing,
and rigid economy in the expenditure of our mental resources.

Let it not be said that in mind, manners, and literature we are
becoming effete, degenerate, and debauched. Let us check, by
determined effort, the spread of those doctrines, false in religion,
medicine, and political economy, tending to the destruction of

our native population, and antagonize, by all the means in our power, the tremendous tide of effeminacy, sensuality, ignorance, folly, and splendid barbarism, which threat us to sweep away our liberties, literature, republican government, and national character.

To do what lies in our sphere, we must restore our profession to the style and rank of learned; we must perpetuate a cordial union with the institutions of learning; we must elevate our standard to the ideal of justice and excellence; we must induce a fair proportion of the *élite* of the youth of the country to enter our ranks, and by literature, conversation, and social influence, cultivate those relations with society which shall enable us to give permanence to ideas of truth, virtue, and justice. We must return, humble and chastened, to the feet of divine philosophy, and acknowledge supernatural charity as the life-giving principle of our art.

Before we speak the word which snaps the spell by which we are bound together; ere we say farewell, and consign the present hour to the foaming wake of the all-absorbing, irreclaimable, ever-swiftly receding past; while we tighten the buckles of our harness and prepare for our departure, let us revert once more to our College, and consider her present interests and future prospects.

Based on an honorable fame; custodian of one of the most celebrated names; graced by youthful, accomplished, and enthusiastic teachers; affiliated with an institution of learning, and associated with science and literature, she is prepared to accomplish a glorious destiny. She will shortly remove to a new habitation, with enlarged and improved facilities; and let us hope that she may ere long become identified with a hospital, and let us not cease in our efforts to obtain this indispensably necessary alliance. Let her imitate in her policy the broad and liberal policy of our civil institutions, and invite to her aid and a share in her honors, learning, ability, and capacity to teach from whatever quarter—native or foreign they may present themselves. May her future be as distinguished as her antecedents have been bold and successful, and become an indestructible portion of the history of an epoch, which, we trust, is about to dawn, of the union of medicine and learning, of philosophy and science, of the *a priori* and the inductive, of the abstract and the concrete, of spirit and matter, and a consequent legitimate material and intellectual progress and development.

But the sun has crossed the meridian and tends toward the western horizon; the tops of the distant mountains are bathed in purple light, and the black shadows at their base begin to creep in a stealthy and hound-like manner over the plain; a rising murmur in the branches of the forest warns us to lift up again our burdens and take our respective roads.

UNIVERSITY OF NEW YORK.

MEDICAL DEPARTMENT.

FACULTY OF MEDICINE.

Rev. ISAAC FERRIS, D. D., LL. D... .*Chancellor of the University.*

MARTYN PAINE, M. D., LL. D...... { *Emeritus Professor of Materia Medica and Therapeutics.*

JOHN W. DRAPER, M. D., LL. D.... { *Emeritus Professor of Chemistry and Physiology.*

ALFRED C. POST, M. D............ { *Professor of the Principles and Operations of Surgery, with Military Surgery and Hygiene.*

CHARLES A. BUDD, M. D......... { *Professor of Obstetrics, with Diseases of Women and Children, and Clinical Midwifery.*

JOHN C. DRAPER, M. D............. *Professor of Chemistry.*

ALFRED L. LOOMIS, M. D......... { *Professor of Institutes and Practice of Medicine.*

WM. DARLING, A. M., M. D., F. R. C. S. { *Professor of General, Descriptive, and Surgical Anatomy.*

HENRY DRAPER, M. D.............. *Professor of Physiology.*

WILLIAM H. THOMSON, M. D...... { *Professor of Materia Medica and Therapeutics.*

J. W. S. GOULEY, M. D............. *Professor of Clinical Surgery.*

ABRAHAM JACOBI, M. D............ *Clinical Prof. of Diseases of Children.*

D. B. St. JOHN ROOSA, M. D....... { *Clinical Professor of Diseases of the Eye and Ear.*

F. D. WEISSE, M. D.................. *Clinical Professor of Dermatology.*

JOHN H. HINTON, M. D .... *Prosector to the Professor of Surgery.*

Z. E. LEWIS, M. D.................... *Assistant Demonstrator of Anatomy.*

JAMES F. FEELEY, M. D............ *Prosector to the Professor of Anatomy.*

M. S. BUTTLES, M. D................ *Assistant to the Professor of Midwifery.*

W. R. GILLETTE, M. D............. { *Assistant to the Professor of Practice of Medicine.*

H. LeB. HARTT, M. D.............. { *Assistant to the Clinical Professor of Diseases of Children.*

CHARLES J. PARDEE, M. D........ { *Assistant to the Clinical Professor of Diseases of the Eye and Ear.*

JOHN W. DRAPER, M. D., LL. D., *President of the Faculty.*

HENRY DRAPER, M. D., *Registrar of the Faculty.*

OFFICERS

Alumni Association of the Medical Department of the University of the City of New York.

— ⚬ —

President.

SAMUEL S. PURPLE, M. D., New York.

Vice-Presidents.

JAMES B. McGRAW, M. D., Wisconsin.
DANIEL AYRES, M. D., New York.
SOLOMON S. SATCHWELL, M. D., North Carolina.
HENRY S. HEWIT, M. D., New York.
FREDERICK D. LENTE, M. D., New York.
JAMES R. LEAMING, M. D., New York.

Secretary.

H. MORTIMER BRUSH, M. D., New York.

Treasurer.

CHAS. J. PARDEE, M. D., New York.

College Historian.

H. M. SPRAGUE, M. D., New York.

Orator for 1868.

HENRY S. HEWIT, M. D., New York.

Committee on Nominations and Arrangements.

D. B. St. JOHN ROOSA, M. D., New York.
J. J. BULL, M. D., "
Z. E. LEWIS, M. D., "
J. H. ANDERSON, M. D., "
WILLIAM B. LEWIS, M. D.,

A catalogue of all the Graduates of the College and a copy of proceedings. Any information or blank diplomas may be had to H. M. Brush, No. 7 West Forty-ninth Street, New York.